POM POM PALS

POMPOM PALS

Easy instructions for creating 14 fuzzy friends

Creatures created by
Michelle Tilly

NH

NEW
HOLLAND

CONTENTS

Published in 2011 by New Holland
Publishers (UK) Ltd
London • Cape Town • Sydney • Auckland
www.newhollandpublishers.com

Garfield House, 86–88 Edgware Road,
London W2 2EA, United Kingdom
80 McKenzie Street, Cape Town 8001,
South Africa
Unit 1, 66 Gibbes Street, Chatswood,
NSW 2067, Australia
218 Lake Road, Northcote,
Auckland, New Zealand

10 9 8 7 6 5 4 3 2 1

A catalogue record for this book is
available from the British Library

ISBN: 978-1-78009-029-0

Printed in China

This book was conceived, designed,
and produced by
Ivy Press
210 High Street, Lewes
East Sussex BN7 2NS, UK
www.ivy-group.co.uk

Creative Director Peter Bridgewater
Publisher Jason Hook
Editorial Director Caroline Earle
Art Director Clare Harris
Senior Project Editor Sophie Collins
Designers Clare Barber and Ginny Zeal
Illustrator Vicky Mitchell
Photographer Andrew Perris

Important!
Pompom pals are not toys. They
are made with small objects that
are choking hazards and are not
suitable for children under 3 years.

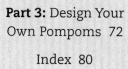

READ THIS FIRST!

Pompoms are simple to make, but these two pages will answer a few important questions before you begin.

HOW ARE POMPOMS MADE?

All the pals and pets in this book are made from between one and three homemade pompoms. The pompoms are made by winding wool around two card circles (detailed steps show you how to do this on pages 8–9), snipping the wool and shaping it. Then you make your chosen pal or pet by adding eyes and felt or fabric features. A freshly made pompom is round, so most are given a haircut with scissors to make them the right shape. Where a pal takes more than one pompom to make, the pompoms are tied together with a spare length of wool. Pompoms are always made with double knitting (DK) wool.

WHAT WILL I NEED?

To make a pompom you'll need a ball of wool to make the body, felt or fabric for the arms and ears, buttons for the eyes and a needle and thread for sewing it together. You'll also need card circle templates for winding the wool. You'll find these templates on pages 10–11. Three sizes are have been supplied for making large, medium and small pompoms. You'll need to cut out two of each size you will be using by photocopying the template and tracing the circles onto thick card. Once you have cut out the card circles you can use them over and over again, replacing them if they get worn or frayed.

HOW SHOULD I START?

If you have some spare wool, make a test pompom before you start your first one. The more practise you have, the neater your pompoms will turn out. We suggest you start your pompom collection with Pompidou, the first pal in the book – she's one of the easiest to make.

DO I NEED TO BE ABLE TO SEW?

Some of the added felt or fabric features are sewn together. If you haven't sewn before, start by threading the needle with a 30-cm- (12-inch)-long length of thread. Tie a knot at the end of the thread, then backstitch (as shown in the diagram below) along the stitching lines shown on the templates.

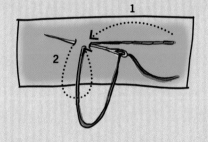

Some of the pals and pets have button eyes to be sewn on. If you're not confident in doing this, you can glue them on instead, using ordinary PVA glue.

HOW DO I USE THE TEMPLATES?

The templates for any features for a pal or pet are shown actual size on the page opposite that pompom's photograph. Trace the templates onto baking parchment, then cut them out and lay them over the felt or fabric to be used. The templates use dotted lines to show the lines you need to sew:

DO I NEED ANY SPECIAL EQUIPMENT?

You will need a pair of sharp scissors (fabric scissors are ideal because they have long, narrow blades, which make it easy to trim the wool to shape, but ordinary sharp scissors will work fine), and some PVA glue to attach features to the pals and pets. That's it.

Now you are ready to make your first pompom!

HOW TO MAKE A POMPOM

The woolly pompom is the basic unit of all the pals. The pals and pets here are made using three sizes of pompom: small (with a 9-cm/3½-inch diameter), medium (with a 10-cm/4¼-inch diameter) and large (with a 12-cm/4¾-inch diameter).

1 Take the two card pompom rings that match the size of pompom you want to make and line them up with one another.

2 Cut the colour or colours of wool you are using into lengths of about 2 m (6 ft) – this will help you avoid tangling your wool. The weights given are suggestions – you may need slightly more or less depending on how tightly you wrap the wool. Holding one end of the wool at the back of the rings, pass the other end through the centre and around the outside edge, then take it back through the centre again. Repeat, working clockwise around the ring until the centre hole is full of wool. Add on new lengths of wool as you go, making sure that the free end is on the outside edge of the ring. If you find it difficult to get the wool through the centre for the final rounds, either push it through firmly with your fingers or thread it on to a large needle to pull it through.

3 Now for the tricky part! Take the fully wound ring and hold it firmly in one hand. Slip the point of your scissors through the loops around the outside and down between the two ring shapes. Snip all the loops of wool carefully, a few at a time.

4 When all the loops have been snipped, carefully ease the rings apart a little. Cut a length of wool 30 cm (12 inches) long and fold it in half. Wrap the wool around the centre and tie tightly in a triple knot. It's very important to make this knot secure, or your pompom will fall apart when you remove the rings.

5 Now gently pull the rings apart to release your pompom. You may find that it looks a little uneven; if so, trim it carefully with a pair of small, sharp scissors.

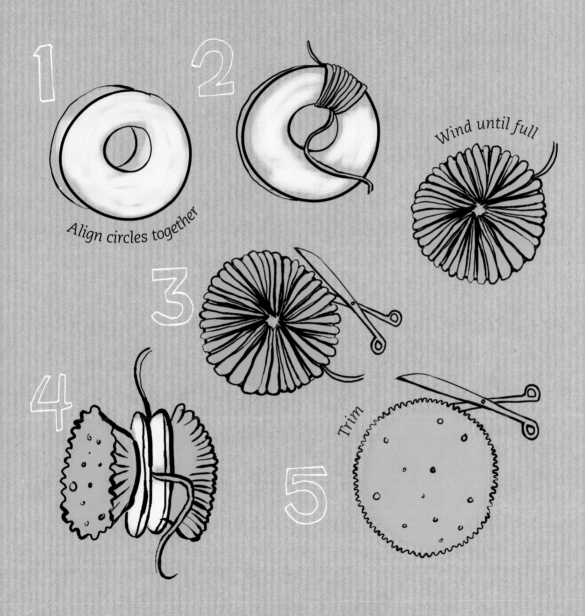

1

Align circles together

2

Wind until full

3

4

Trim

5

POMPOM TEMPLATES

Large pompom

Medium pompom

Small pompom

PART ONE

POMPOM PALS

POMPIDOU

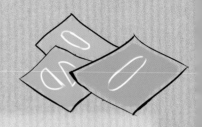

There's something pleasing about the expression of this little pal. Maybe it's her high-contrast colours or her strange double mouth. There's a hint of the unusual about her – something just slightly off-kilter. Whatever it is, she's a smart addition to the pompom menagerie – and she's one of the easiest creatures in the whole zoo to make.

YOU WILL NEED

* 115 g (4 oz) red wool

* 2 mismatched buttons in contrasting sizes and colours

* Scraps of green, grey and turquoise felt

* Small quantity of wadding, cotton wool or other stuffing

* Needle and coloured sewing thread

* Sharp scissors

* PVA glue

Outer mouth

Inner mouth

Right ear

Left ear

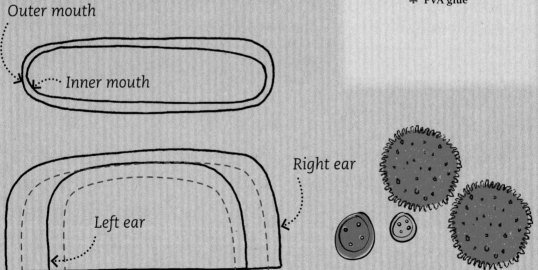

TO MAKE POMPIDOU

1 Make two medium-sized pompoms from red wool as shown on pages 8–9.

2 Tie the pompoms around the centre with a piece of wool, then knot tightly and trim the ends. Fluff the pompoms up around the tie and trim any scruffy pieces of wool.

3 Using a pair of sharp scissors and following the photograph on page 15, cut Pompidou into shape. Snip small pieces, using the blades of the scissors rather than the points, and work on getting the surfaces flat and even and the corners softly rounded.

4 When you are happy with Pompidou's shape, sew on her eyes. Thread the needle and stitch each eye firmly into place, sewing deep into the centre of the pompom. Knot the threads into the pompom and trim the ends.

5 Add the ears. Trace the template on page 14 onto baking parchment, cut around the shape and use it to cut four ear shapes from green felt. Sew around the stitching lines, either using a sewing machine or a small backstitch as shown on page 5, then turn the ears right side out so that you have two small 'pockets'. Stuff them slightly with cotton wool and stitch the openings closed. Glue each ear in position. Prop and leave to dry.

6 Finally, add the mouth. Use the templates on page 14 to cut out two shapes for the mouth from baking parchment, then cut the inner mouth shape from grey felt and the outer mouth shape from turquoise. Stitch firmly in place on the face, using just a stitch or two and passing the needle through the centre of the pompom. Knot the thread into the pompom and trim the end.

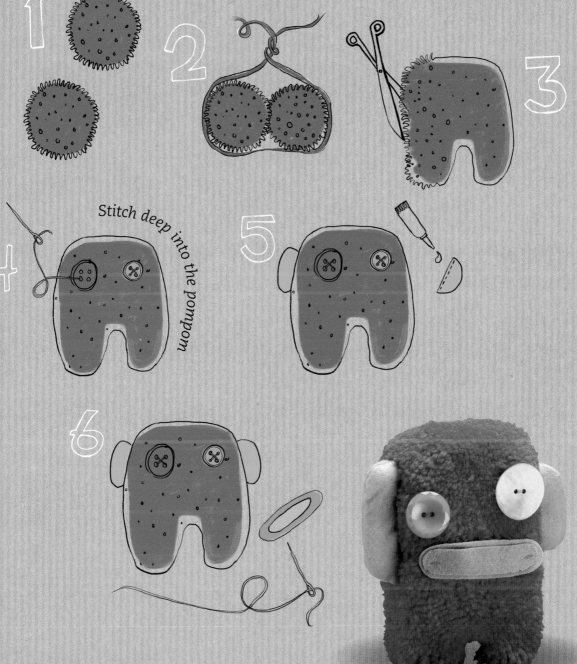

Stitch deep into the pompom

LULU

Round and cuddly, Lulu is a chunky pal in brilliant red. Her wide-set button eyes and neat little patterned ears give her a friendly look. She's quick to make – just one medium pompom, trimmed and tweaked, plus one or two cheerful finishing touches.

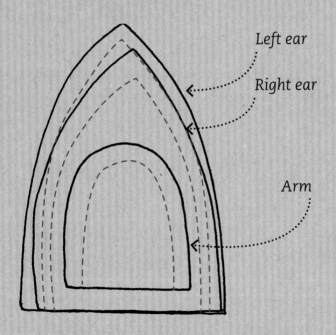

Left ear

Right ear

Arm

YOU WILL NEED

* 55 g (2 oz) bright red wool

* 2 medium-sized dark buttons

* Scraps of blue felt

* Scraps of patterned material for Lulu's ears

* Small quantity of wadding, cotton wool or other stuffing

* Needle and coloured sewing thread

* Sharp scissors

* PVA glue

TO MAKE LULU

1 Make a medium-sized pompom in bright red wool as shown on pages 8–9. Lulu sits on a flat base, so trim one side of the round pompom to help her to sit upright. Use the sides of the scissor blades, not the points, and cut slowly and carefully – this makes it easier to get a flat edge.

2 Make baking parchment templates for the ears and arms as described on page 7. Cut four arm shapes out of the blue felt. Sew each pair of pieces neatly around the stitching line to make two pockets, either by hand or machine (if you are sewing by hand, use a small backstitch). Turn the arms right side out and stuff them with a little wadding or cotton wool stuffing. Sew the open ends shut.

3 Using the patterned material, cut two left and two right ear shapes. You can use the same material for both ears, or pick something different for each ear – it's up to you. As with the arms, sew each pair of ear shapes together along the stitching lines on the template, right sides in, either by hand or machine, then turn the ears right side out, stuff them lightly and sew the open ends closed.

4 Sew on the buttons for Lulu's eyes. Her expression depends on her eyes being placed quite wide apart, so experiment with different positions before you sew. When you are happy with how they look, sew them on using coloured thread, sewing deeply through the centre of the pompom. Knot the thread into Lulu's body and tie off the end.

5 Finally, add Lulu's arms and ears. Look at the photograph on page 19 to determine where to place them. Put a dab of glue on the sewn end of each arm and place them deep into the pompom, parting the wool to get to the centre. Leave until the glue is dry, then attach Lulu's ears in the same way. Sit her upright on a flat surface until the glue is dry and her ears are fixed.

Sew into the centre of Lulu's body

VEGGIEPOM

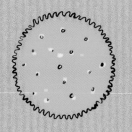

Veggiepom's head is a little bigger than her body, so she looks like a friendly mushroom. With her cheerful mixture of colours and invitingly outstretched arms, she makes a good pocket pal. She also works well in lots of other colour mixtures – if you wish, try making her in light blue and bright red, or in brown and dark blue.

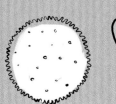

YOU WILL NEED

* 30 g (1 oz) white wool

* 30 g (1 oz) pink wool

* 30 g (1 oz) gold wool

* 2 mismatched buttons in contrasting sizes and colours

* Scraps of grey, bright pink and bright green felt

* Needle and coloured sewing thread

* Sharp scissors

* PVA glue

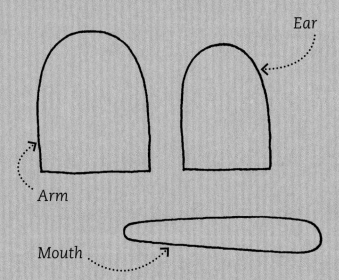

Ear

Arm

Mouth

TO MAKE VEGGIEPOM

1 Make one small pompom in white wool and one medium-sized one in pink-and-gold mix, following the directions on pages 8–9. You make a mixed-colour pompom by winding two strands of wool, one of each colour, around the card centre at once. Use a length of the leftover wool to tie the two pompoms together around their middles. Knot it tightly and trim the ends. Fluff the pompoms up around the wool (this will bring any straggly ends to the surface and make the pompom easier to trim).

2 Using the photograph on page 23 as a guide, trim the smaller pompom into a short, thick 'stem' shape, and cut the pink and gold pompom so that it has a flat underside, giving it an 'edge' where it meets the white pompom. Snip neatly and slowly, holding your pal up regularly to check its shape.

3 Decide where you want the eyes to go and, using a sewing needle threaded with matching thread, sew them one by one into the top pompom, stitching through the middle of the ball. Knot the threads in the middle of the pompom, then trim the ends with scissors.

4 Make baking parchment templates from the outlines on page 22. Cut out one mouth from the green felt, two ears from the pink felt and two arms from the grey felt. Use the glue to attach the mouth in place, positioning it carefully. Put a little dab of glue along the bottom edge of each ear shape and place the ears deeply into the pompom towards the back of the head.

5 Place the felt arms on either side of Veggiepom by putting a dab of glue on the flat end of each arm and placing them deeply into her body. Leave Veggiepom propped up until the glue is completely dry.

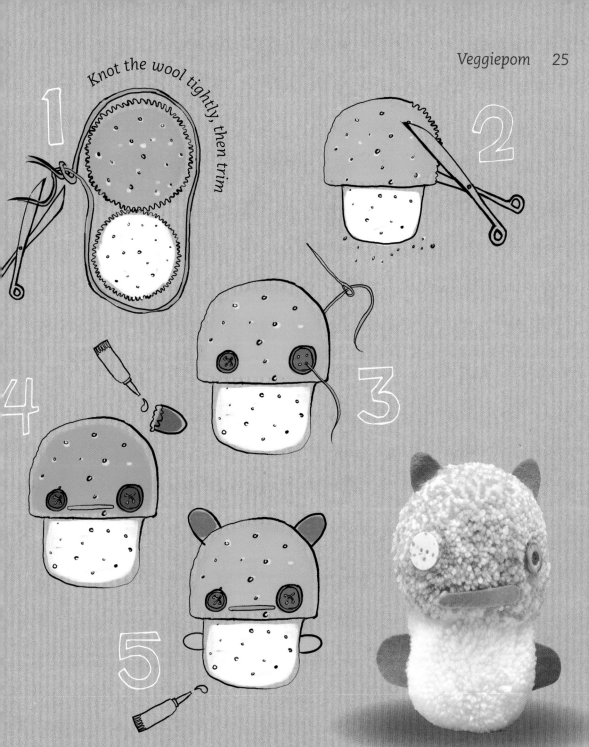

Knot the wool tightly, then trim

SNOWPOM

Is she a snow-woman or the Abominable Snowpom? You can't really tell from this little creature's expression, but her odd cork and snap fastener eyes give her character. And if you think she looks cold, you could always add a miniature wool scarf, or knit her some mitts!

YOU WILL NEED

* 115 g (4 oz) white wool
* 1 medium-sized press stud fastener
* 1 cork 'dot' *(you can find cards of these in craft shops)*
* Scraps of white felt
* Small quantity of wadding, cotton wool or other stuffing
* Needle and white sewing thread
* Sharp scissors
* PVA glue

Arm

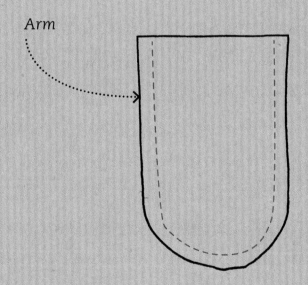

TO MAKE SNOWPOM

1 Make two medium-sized pompoms in white wool as shown on pages 8–9. You may find that they don't require the full amount of wool – stop when the card rings are tightly filled. Tie them together around the centres with a length of leftover wool and knot the ends tightly. Fluff the pompoms up to bring any straggly ends to the surface, then trim them.

2 Trim Snowpom to the rounded shape with short legs as shown in the photograph on page 27, cutting carefully with the sides of the scissor blades rather than the points. Make the tall shape with a rounded end for the head first, then trim to make a flat base so Snowpom can stand upright. Carefully cut up from the base to create Snowpom's legs.

3 Make the arms – cut four arm shapes from the white felt, using an arm template made from baking parchment and the outline on page 26. Sew around the stitching lines to make two pockets with open ends. You can sew the arms by hand or use a sewing machine. If you are sewing by hand, use a small backstitch as shown in the illustration on page 7. Pad them slightly with a little stuffing, then stitch the open ends closed.

4 Attach Snowpom's arms – run a line of glue along the flat end of one arm and place it deep into Snowpom's side, checking with the photograph on page 27 for the correct placement. Leave the first arm to dry before attaching the second.

5 Add the eyes – place generous dabs of glue on the backs of the cork dot and the press stud fastener and put in place on Snowpom's face. Leave to dry, then smooth down Snowpom with your hands, as if you were stroking a live pet – this will bring any odd ends of wool to the surface and you can snip them off to give her a neat outline.

ROBOPOM

With his asymmetric eyes, wavy black antennae and bold colour scheme, Robopom is a cross between a pompom robot and a well-loved teddy bear. The perfect pal for a one-on-one conversation at the end of a bad day, he's based on three pompoms, one in each of our three sizes, and each in a different colour.

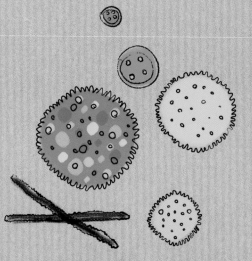

YOU WILL NEED

* 85 g (3 oz) multicoloured wool
* 55 g (2 oz) turquoise wool
* 30 g (1 oz) grey wool
* 2 buttons in contrasting sizes and colours
* 2 thick black craft pipe cleaners
* Needle and sewing thread in colours to match the buttons
* Sharp scissors
* PVA glue

TO MAKE ROBOPOM

1 Make three pompoms according to the directions given on pages 8–9 – a small grey one, a medium-sized turquoise one and a large one using the multicoloured wool.

2 Stack the pompoms, turquoise on top, multicoloured in the middle and grey on the bottom. Tie a length of wool around all three as shown. Knot it tightly to hold the pompoms in place, then trim the ends. Fluff the pompoms up around the wool so that they look even and symmetrical and trim any odd ends that come to the surface.

3 Now trim the pompoms into shape, referring closely to the photograph on page 31. Work slowly, with sharp scissors, getting the edges of the top and base cylinder shapes as sharp and even as you can. Don't trim away too much at a time until you are confident that you are cutting evenly and in straight lines.

4 When your pompom robot is the right shape, sew on his eyes. Thread the needle with the matching coloured thread and stitch through the button's holes and right through the centre of the pompom. Knot the thread deeply into the pompom and then trim the ends. Repeat for the second eye, using the matching colour of thread.

5 Finally, add the antennae. Curl each pipe cleaner loosely into shape (checking with the photograph on page 31), leaving only about 2.5 cm (1 inch) at each end. Cut off any extra pipe cleaner length beyond this. Dab some glue on to the base end of one pipe cleaner and insert the glued end deep into the top pompom. Repeat with the other antenna. Prop your pompom robot upright where he won't be disturbed until the glue is fully dry.

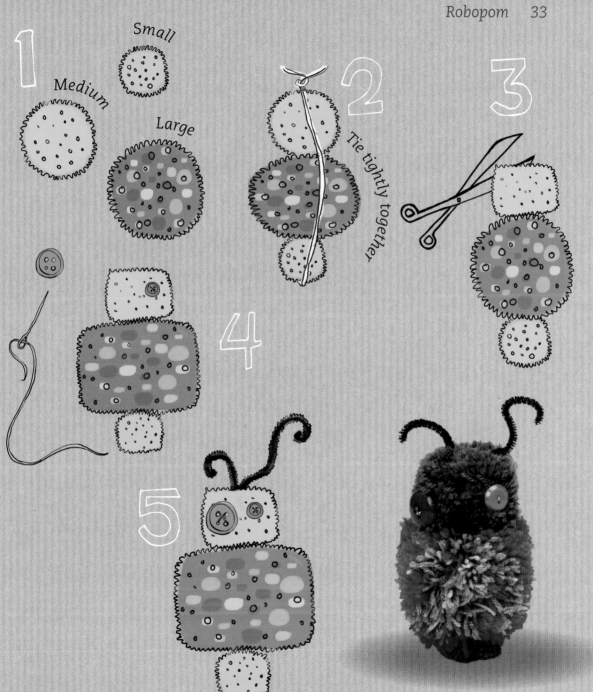

1

Medium
Small
Large

2

Tie tightly together

3

4

5

ODDPOM

Oddpom's metal bobbin eyes and wide, toothy grin give him an instant cuddly charm. He is easily made with two medium-sized pompoms, although you may need a little practise in trimming to get his sides absolutely even.

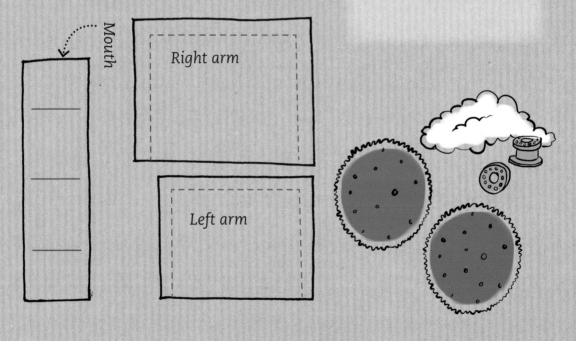

Mouth

Right arm

Left arm

TO MAKE ODDPOM

1 Make two medium-sized pompoms from red wool following the instructions on pages 8–9. Tie the pompoms around the middle with a spare length of wool, knotting the wool deeply into the pompoms and trimming the ends. Fluff up the joined pompoms a little and trim any straggly ends with scissors. Cut Oddpom's shape carefully – start by cutting a flat base, then cut a flat top to his head using the blades of the scissors rather than the points. Cut the straight sides of Oddpom and, when you have an upright rectangular shape, cut the small curve that divides his base into two legs.

2 Make the arm templates from baking parchment using the outlines on page 34, then cut two right-arm shapes from the green felt and two left-arm ones from the blue. Make the arms by sewing around the stitching lines of each pair, then turn them right side out to make two pockets with open ends. You can sew the arms by hand or use a sewing machine; if you are sewing by hand, use a small backstitch. Fill – not too tightly – with a little stuffing, then stitch the open ends closed.

3 Attach the arms by gluing along one long side of each arm and placing it deep into the middle of Oddpom's side.

4 Cut the mouth out of yellow felt following the mouth template on page 34. Thread a needle with the blue embroidery cotton and make three long stitches where marked on the template, knotting the cotton on the wrong side. Run a line of glue around the wrong edge of the mouth and put the mouth in place just above the arms.

5 Add Oddpom's eyes by carefully brushing glue on one side of each metal bobbin and positioning the bobbins on Oddpom's face. Lay him on his back to allow the glue to dry. To finish, stroke Oddpom gently all over to bring any odd ends of wool to the surface and trim if necessary to make his body smooth.

Stitch mouth loosely

WAVER

This enthusiastic orange pal looks as if he is jumping for joy. Be especially sure to look at the photograph when you are carefully shaping the top of his head – his ear bumps need to be cut just right for him to have this cheery look!

YOU WILL NEED

* 115 g (4 oz) bright orange wool
* 2 small mismatched buttons *(bright colours work best)*
* 2 squares, 15 x 15 cm (6 x 6 inches) each, of orange felt
* Small quantity of wadding, cotton wool or other stuffing
* Needle and orange sewing thread
* Sharp scissors
* PVA glue

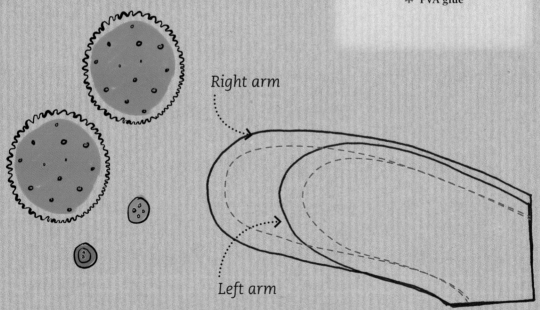

Right arm

Left arm

TO MAKE WAVER

1 Make two medium-sized pompoms from orange wool as shown on pages 8–9. Tie them together around their centres with a leftover piece of wool, knot the wool deep into the centre of a pompom and trim the ends.

2 Cut Waver's body to shape. He is a flat-fronted upright rectangle with a leg at each lower corner and an ear at each upper one, so start by cutting straight sides, using the blades of the scissors rather than the points. When Waver's sides are straight, cut a flat front and back. Finally, cut a shallow curve across the top of the head, leaving the ears standing up at the corners, and cut another gentle curve at the bottom of Waver to make his legs.

3 Make arm templates using baking parchment and following the templates on page 38. Cut two pieces for each of Waver's arm shapes from the orange felt. Sew around the stitching lines of each, either using a sewing machine or by hand. If you are sewing by hand, use a small backstitch.

4 Turn the arm pockets right side out and stuff them quite tightly with cotton wool or wadding. They should be well padded. Sew the open ends closed. Put a generous line of glue along the stitched end of each arm and place the arms deeply into Waver's sides, using the photograph on page 39 to help you put them in the right place. Prop Waver against a solid surface and leave him until the glue is completely dry.

5 Finally, add Waver's eyes. They should be quite close to the sides of his face and placed just above his arms. Put a dab of glue on the back of each button and gently place them, then leave Waver resting on his back until the glue is completely dry and he can stand right side up, waving happily to the world.

1

2

3

Use a needle to help turn Waver's arms right side out

4

5

PART TWO

POMPOM PETS

OWLY

With outstretched wings and a pretty patterned beak, Owly is one of the easiest pets to make. Try different buttons for the eyes to get the best look for your owl, but remember that they should be big to get the right owl effect.

YOU WILL NEED

* 55 g (2 oz) bright blue wool
* 2 large mismatched buttons
* Scraps of deep green and pink felt
* Scrap of patterned fabric
* Small quantity of wadding, cotton wool or other stuffing
* Needle and coloured sewing thread
* Sharp scissors
* PVA glue

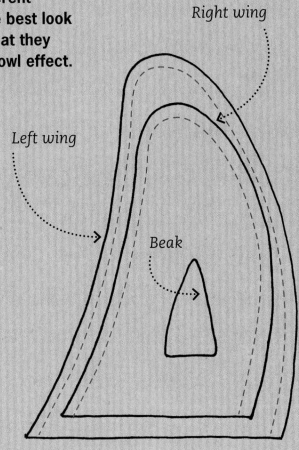

Right wing

Left wing

Beak

TO MAKE OWLY

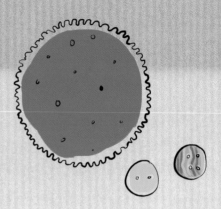

1 Make a medium-sized pompom from blue wool, following the instructions on pages 8–9. Fluff up the pompom to bring any straggly ends to the surface, then trim them. Carefully cut the pompom to a slightly oval shape with a flat base so that Owly will stand up. Use the sides of the scissor blades, not the points, and cut slowly and carefully.

2 Make two wing templates from baking parchment, one for the right wing and one for the left, using the outlines on page 44. Cut out two left wings from the green felt and two right wings from the pink. Sew them along the stitching lines. You can sew the wings by hand or use a sewing machine. If you are sewing by hand, use a small backstitch as shown in the illustration on page 7. Turn the wings right side out (trim the points to avoid bunching at the tips), and fill with a little wadding or cotton wool stuffing. Sew the open ends closed.

3 Make a beak template from baking parchment and cut out two beak pieces from the patterned fabric. Glue the pieces together with a little glue at the straight end, then leave to dry.

4 Sew on the eyes, using contrasting thread and sewing deep into the pompom. Knot the thread into the pompom and trim the ends.

5 Glue on the wings and the beak, using lines of glue at the straight edges of each, and place them carefully – use the position of the eyes as a guide. When the glue is dry, smooth down Owly's body and snip off any stray ends of wool that emerge.

Use 3 or 4 stitches for each eye

POPPET

Poppet has a modest humble look despite his jolly vivid-blue body. Take the time to cut his shape neatly – because he only has eyes and little legs to give him personality, they need to be carefully placed, and any straggly wool ends should be trimmed to make his shape as round and smooth as possible.

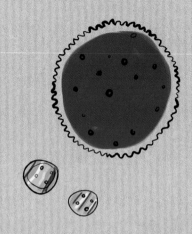

YOU WILL NEED

* 55 g (2 oz) bright blue wool

* 2 tortoiseshell buttons, one a little larger than the other

* Sharp scissors

* PVA glue

TO MAKE POPPET

1 Make a medium-sized pompom from bright blue wool as shown on pages 8–9. Smooth it down with your hands to bring any straggly ends to the surface and trim it to make it as round and tidy as possible.

2 Start to make Poppet's shape by carefully cutting a flat base for him to stand on. (You'll be dividing it into legs in a minute.) Do not cut too deeply into the pompom – the base should be small, because you don't want to spoil the roundness of the shape overall.

3 When you have a small flat area on which your pompom can stand upright, cut a little more wool away from Poppet's front and back. Snip carefully and gently, using the blades of the scissors rather than the points, and don't cut too much off – you're trying to give Poppet a slight curve down to the legs, not a sharp angle.

4 Finally, cut about 1.5 cm (½ inch) up from the middle of the flat base of the pompom to create the legs. They should be short, so don't cut too deeply into the pompom. Trim away the wool until there is about a 1.5-cm (½-inch) space between them, and neaten up any ends. Check as you cut to make sure that Poppet can still stand upright on his feet.

5 Add the eyes. Try various positions – to make Poppet's modest expression they should be stuck slightly on the undercurve of the pompom. When you are sure you know where you want them placed, put a dab of glue on the back of each button and stick them in place. Leave Poppet resting on his back until the glue is completely dry, then stroke him all over with your hands (as if you were stroking a live pet) to bring any last straggly ends of wool to the surface. Trim any that you find.

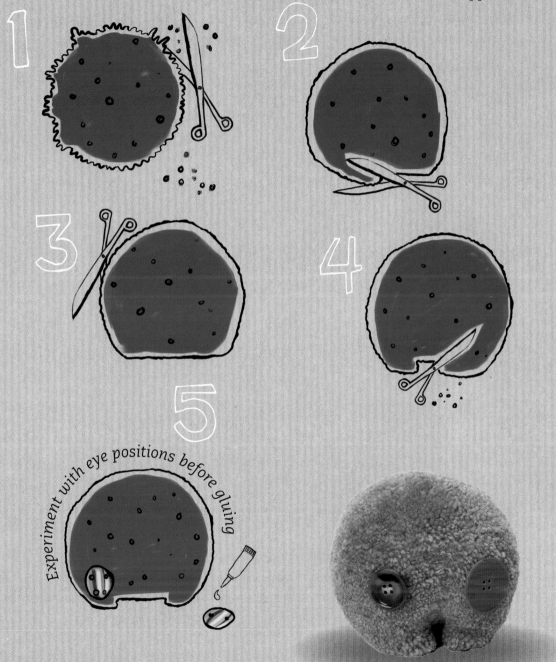

Experiment with eye positions before gluing

CYCLOPS

Like the giant in the ancient Greek
story, Cyclops only has one eye,
but our pet makes up for it with two
antennae with lovely round green ends.
His multicoloured freckles are made
by winding a last layer of multicoloured
wool around the outside of the pompom
just before it is finished.

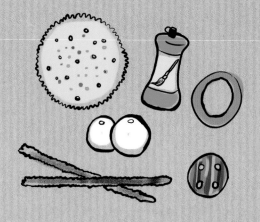

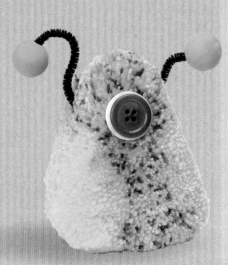

YOU WILL NEED

* 55 g (2 oz) golden-yellow wool

* 5.5 m (18 ft) multicoloured wool

* 1 large silver washer
(you can get this from a DIY centre)

* 1 button, a little smaller
than the washer

* 2 thick black craft
pipe cleaners

* 2 large plastic beads

* Green poster paint

* Sharp scissors

* PVA glue

TO MAKE CYCLOPS

1 Make a medium-sized pompom from golden-yellow wool as shown on pages 8–9. When the card circle is almost completely filled with wool, change to the multicoloured wool for the last bit of wrapping. Make sure that the end of the multicoloured wool hangs on the outside edge of the pompom disc, rather than the inner one, so that you can trim off the rough end of the wool while you are cutting the pompom to shape. Finish the pompom and fluff it up to bring any straggly ends to the surface.

2 Cut the pompom into Cyclops's triangular shape, using the blades of the scissors rather than the points. The easiest way to do this is to cut the flat base first, then very gradually work upward swith long but shallow cuts, using the scissor blades to shape the triangle. Work slowly – if you make any cuts that go too deep, you will spoil the pompom and have to start again.

3 Add Cyclops's eye. Glue the button to the washer, leaving an even rim all around it. When the glue has dried, place the eye on Cyclops and glue it into place.

4 Paint the plastic beads green. When the paint is dry, gently push one end of a pipe cleaner into the centre of each bead.

5 Trim the pipe cleaners to a length that you like and bend them into the squiggly shape you need for the antennae, using the photograph on page 53 as a guide. Put a generous dab of glue on the end of each pipe cleaner and press into place deep in the sides of Cyclops's head. Leave them to dry, then stroke Cyclops gently to bring any odd ends of wool to the surface. Trim the ends to make his shape smooth and even.

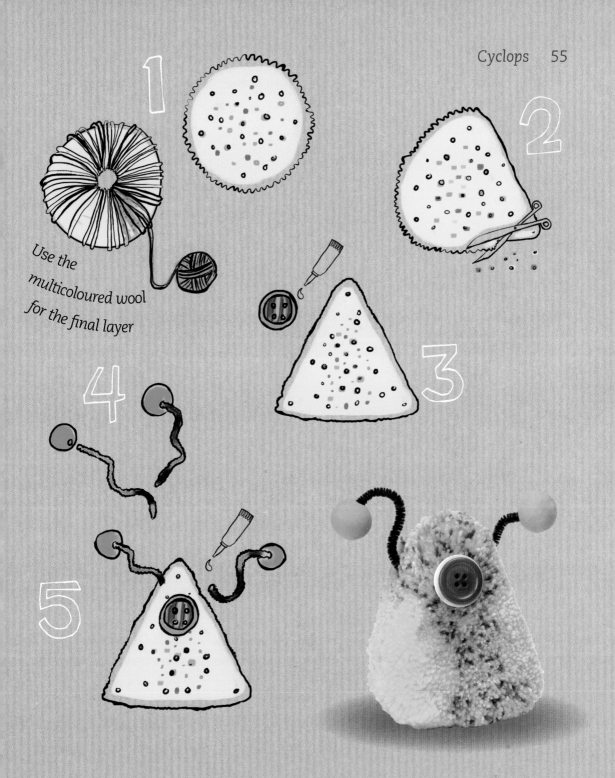

Use the multicoloured wool for the final layer

MOBY

Swimming up from the ocean depths, Moby has a body made from one large pompom in a rich green-blue wool. His tail is made from grey felt, and he has a squiggly water spout twisted from a black pipe cleaner. One big dark eye and one tiny light one give him a rather puzzled expression.

YOU WILL NEED

* 85 g (3 oz) deep green-blue wool
* 5.5 m (18 ft) multicoloured wool
* 2 mismatched buttons
* 2 squares, 15 x 15 cm (6 x 6 inches) each, of grey felt
* Small quantity of wadding, cotton wool or other stuffing
* 1 thick black craft pipe cleaner
* Needle and grey sewing thread
* Sharp scissors
* PVA glue

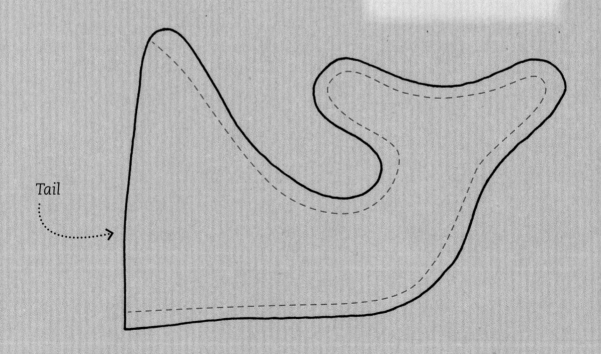

Tail

TO MAKE MOBY

1 Make a large-sized pompom of the green-blue wool as shown on pages 8–9. Add one 5.5-m (18-ft) length of multicoloured wool last on the disc when it is almost full to create the speckled effect on Moby's sides. Carefully trim the pompom to shape, using the photograph on page 57 as a guide. Snip a little at a time until you are happy with Moby's outline. He should sit upright on a flat base.

2 Make Moby's tail. Make a template from baking parchment using the outline on page 56, then cut two tail shapes from the grey felt. Sew around the stitching line on the template with grey thread (you can sew this by hand or machine; if you are sewing by hand, use the backstitch).

3 Turn the tail right side out. You can use a blunt needle to help push out the corners of the tail. Press the tail lightly with a warm iron and pad it with stuffing. Use the point of the scissors to push little pieces of stuffing into the corners of the tail, and gradually fill it. It should be padded, but not very tightly stuffed. When the tail is full, neatly sew the opening at the end with grey thread.

4 Attach the tail to Moby with glue. Place a generous line of glue along the body end of the tail, then part the wool at the side of Moby's body and set the glued end deep inside the pompom. Prop Moby carefully and leave the glue to dry.

5 Finally, add Moby's eyes and spout. Place the eyes carefully on Moby's body and fix with small dabs of glue. Twist the pipe cleaner into a spiral shape. Make a little flattened ring at the end where it will attach to Moby's head. Place a little glue on the ring and position it deep into the pompom. Leave the glue to dry for an hour, then smooth Moby with your hands (as though you were stroking a pet) to give him a smooth finish. Trim off any rough ends of wool.

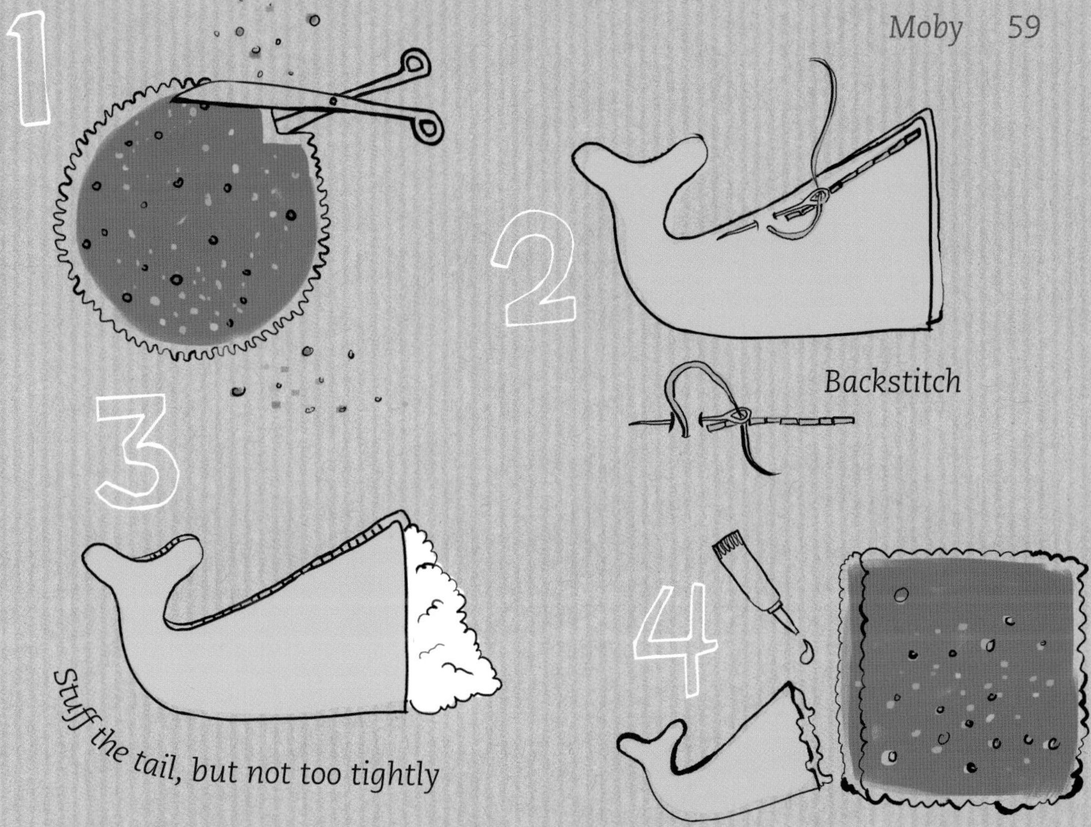

1

2

Backstitch

3

Stuff the tail, but not too tightly

4

5

RABBIT

Rabbit's double ears are tilted slightly forwards as if she is listening closely, and her eyes are particularly close to the sides of her face, so that she can easily see all around her.

YOU WILL NEED

* ✳ 55 g (2 oz) grey wool
* ✳ 85 g (3 oz) orange wool
* ✳ 2 medium mismatched buttons, one light and one dark
* ✳ Scraps of pale blue and deep pink felt
* ✳ 1 square, 15 x 15 cm (6 x 6 inches), of grey felt
* ✳ Needle and grey sewing thread
* ✳ Sharp scissors
* ✳ PVA glue

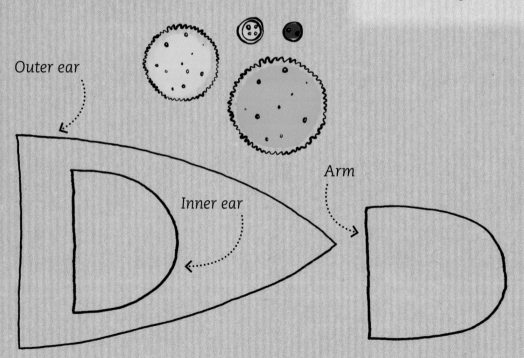

Outer ear

Inner ear

Arm

TO MAKE RABBIT

1 Make one medium-sized grey pompom and one large orange one as shown on pages 8–9. Tie them together around their centres with a leftover piece of wool. Knot the wool tightly in one of the pompoms and trim the ends. Fluff up the pompoms lightly with your hands and trim any straggly ends that come to the surface. The grey pompom making the head should stay round, but the orange one for the body should be trimmed carefully to a rectangular shape. Start by trimming a flat base at the opposite end to the head, then cut two flat sides up to the head and finally trim the front and back of Rabbit to flat surfaces. Work slowly, and use the blades of the scissors rather than the points. When you are happy with the shape, smooth Rabbit with your hands and trim off any odd ends of wool.

2 Make the ear templates from baking parchment using the outlines on page 60, and cut one outer ear shape from the pink felt and one from the blue. Cut two inner ears from grey felt. Lay one inner ear over each outer, matching the lower edges, and fold the shape in half. Sew through the centre back of each double piece to give the ear a slight crease. Knot the thread and trim the ends.

3 Place a line of glue along both lower sides of each ear and place deeply into the top of Rabbit's head. Allow to dry.

4 Add the eyes – check the photograph on page 61 to make sure they are in the right place. Add a dab of glue on the back of each button and set in place. Leave Rabbit on her back until the glue is dry.

5 Make an arm template and cut two arms from the grey felt. Add a line of glue on each side of the flat end of each arm, then place it into the side of the body, about halfway down. When the glue has fully dried, smooth Rabbit all over and trim any ends of wool until she is completely smooth.

EGGHEAD

Egghead is so intelligent that his head is the biggest part of his body. In fact it's the only part of his body, with button eyes set quite low on his huge skull. He is supported by two strong little legs, tightly stuffed to hold him upright.

YOU WILL NEED

* 115 g (4 oz) mixed pink and gold wool

* 2 mismatched tortoiseshell buttons, one large and one small

* Scraps of patterned cotton fabric for the legs

* Small quantity of wadding, cotton wool or other stuffing

* Sharp scissors

* PVA glue

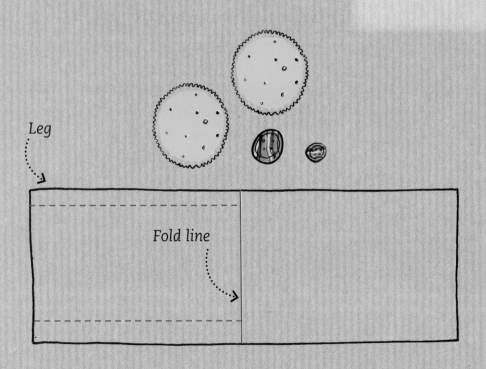

Leg

Fold line

TO MAKE EGGHEAD

1 Make two medium-sized pompoms from pink and gold wool as shown on page 8–9. Tie them together around their centres with a length of leftover wool, knot it tightly deep in one of the pompoms and trim the ends. Fluff the pompoms with your hands to bring any odd ends of wool to the surface, then trim.

2 Trim the joined pompoms to make the Egghead shape. Start by cutting a flat 'face' surface on the front and back, then cut carefully around the sides to make Egghead a flat, deep oval shape, narrowing slightly towards the top of his head. Cut slowly and carefully, using the blades of the scissors rather than the points. Cut a flat base for Egghead.

3 Make Egghead's leg template from baking parchment using the leg outline on page 64. Cut out two leg shapes from the patterned fabric. Fold each piece in half, right side of the fabric facing inwards. Stitch carefully along the stitching lines, either using a sewing machine or by hand. If hand-sewing, use a backstitch as shown on page 7. Leave the end of each leg open, like a pocket, for stuffing.

4 Turn the legs right side out and stuff them tightly through the open ends. They must be strongly stuffed to provide enough support for Egghead to stand upright. When they are full, turn the open ends in and stitch them closed. Run a line of glue along the stitched end of each and carefully position them deep into the underside of Egghead's body. Leave Egghead on his back until the glue is completely dry and his legs are well secured.

5 Finally, add Egghead's eyes. Dab a little glue on the back of each button and place them low on the head to give Egghead his clever expression. When the glue is dry, you can stand Egghead up – his legs will support him. Stroke him gently (as though you were stroking a pet) and trim any rough ends to make his coat smooth.

Lay Egghead on his back to dry

ANTEATER

Anteater is the most difficult-to-make pompom pet in this book. Try him after you have already successfully made a few of the simpler ones. His body and nose are made from three pompoms, two medium and one large, which must be very carefully trimmed to get the right shape.

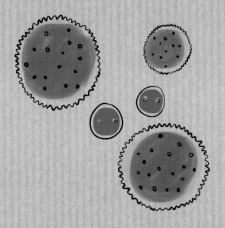

Ear

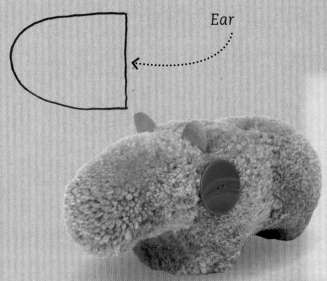

YOU WILL NEED

✳ 140 g (5 oz) grey wool

✳ 2 over-sized buttons in a bright colour

✳ Scraps of grey felt for the ears

✳ Sharp scissors

✳ PVA glue

TO MAKE ANTEATER

1 Make one small and two medium-sized pompoms from grey wool as shown on pages 8–9. Fluff each pompom with your hands and carefully trim any straggly ends that come to the surface. Tie the two medium-sized pompoms together around the centre. Knot the wool tightly deep in one of the pompoms and trim the ends. Gently fluff the pompoms again and trim any straggly ends that you find.

2 Begin to make Anteater's shape from the two joined pompoms by carefully cutting a flat broad back, then working down to form a round curvy bottom. Cut up about 2.5 cm (1 inch) through the middle of the underbelly, leaving 2.5 cm (1 inch) on either side to form the legs. Anteater's sides are slightly smaller and narrower than his shoulders, so cut them in slightly beyond the shoulder.

3 Once the body shape is developed, add the smaller pompom to Anteater in the usual way – by using a length of wool to tie around the centre of the anteater shape and the centre of the smaller pompom. The small pompom will be Anteater's snout, so it needs to be attached at the front.

4 When the small pompom is securely tied, cut it into a long funnel nose shape. Make sure that there is a curve downwards to the front feet in the shape as you cut. Keep looking at the photograph on page 69 to check that the shape is a good match.

5 Add the eyes and ears. Make a template for the ears from baking parchment using the outline on page 68, and cut out in felt. Glue both sides of the flat end of each and place the ears deep in the pompom at either side of the top of the head. Allow to dry. Place a large dab of glue on the wrong side of each button and place them on the sides of Anteater's face just below and in front of the ears. Allow to dry, then smooth your pal a final time and trim any uneven ends of wool sticking out.

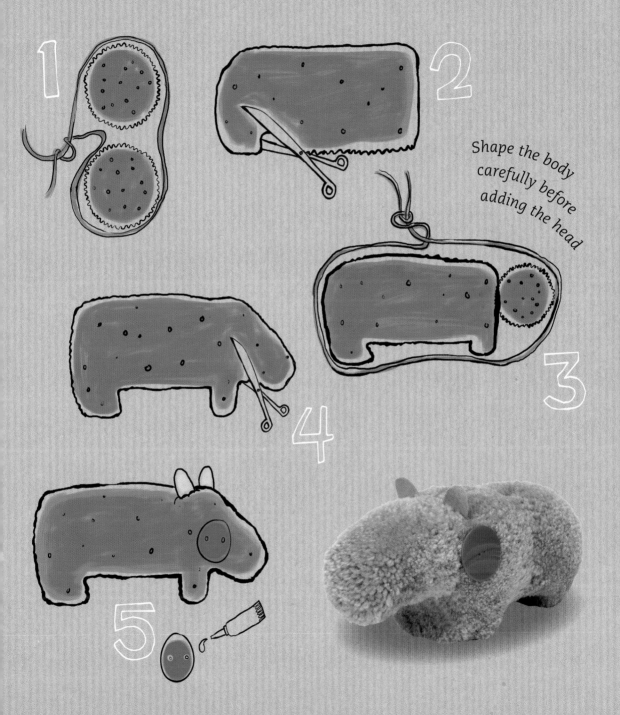

Shape the body
carefully before
adding the head

PART THREE

DESIGN YOUR OWN POMPOMS

DESIGN YOUR OWN POMPOMS

Now that you've mastered the skill of pompom-making, you can branch out and invent some cute new pals and pets of your own.

This section provides inspiration for making some unique creatures. The templates here provide a variety of features for new pompoms. Experiment with funny mixes – add antennae to a rabbit, or big ears to a bird. And, most important of all, try out different positions for the eyes and mouth on any design – these features give a new pal or pet its personality. In addition you could use big coloured buttons instead of little dull ones, vary the colours and shapes of the felt features (arms, mouths, wings, ears and so on) or even use a heavier weight of wool to make rougher, shaggier pompoms.

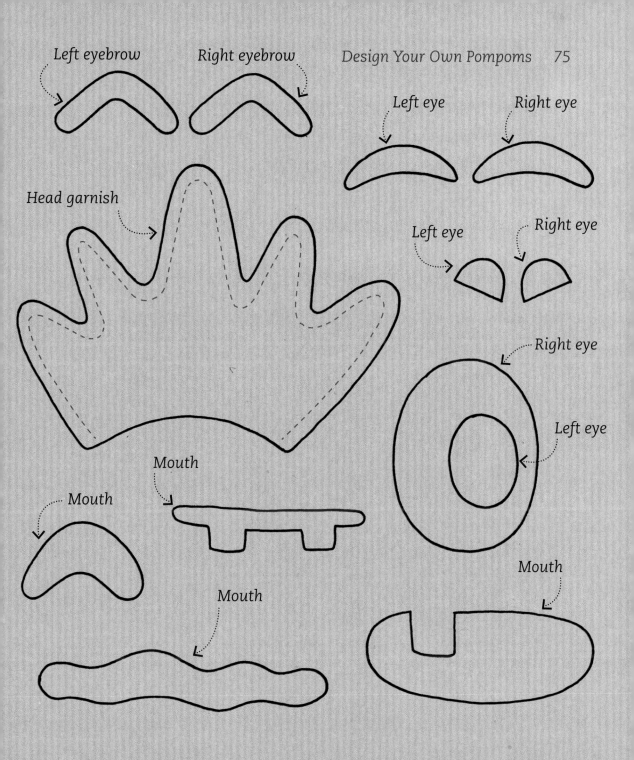

Left eyebrow

Right eyebrow

Left eye

Right eye

Head garnish

Left eye

Right eye

Right eye

Left eye

Mouth

Mouth

Mouth

Mouth

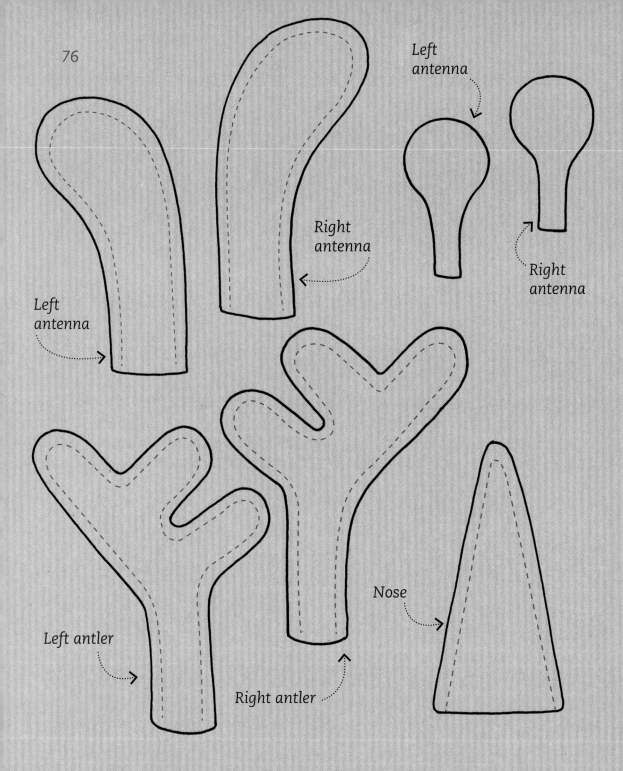

Left
antenna

Right
antenna

Left
antenna

Right
antenna

Left antler

Right antler

Nose

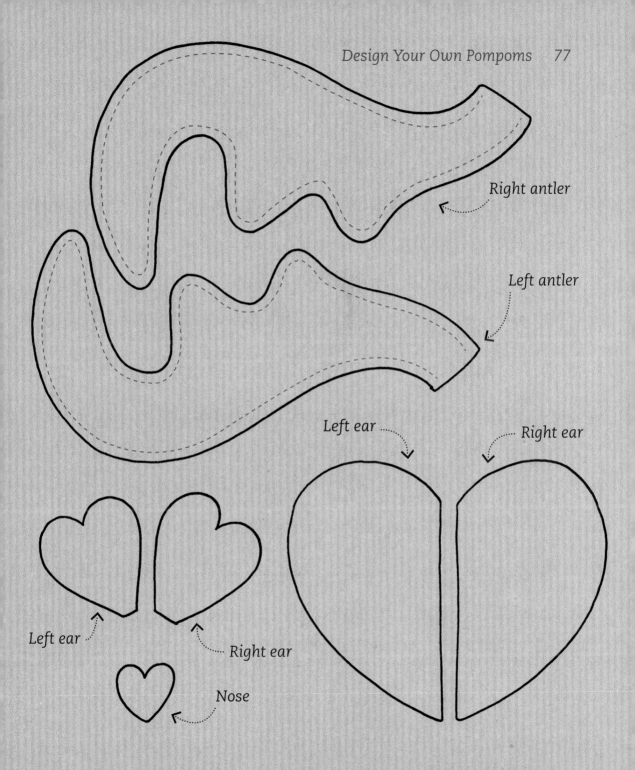

Right antler

Left antler

Left ear

Right ear

Left ear

Right ear

Nose

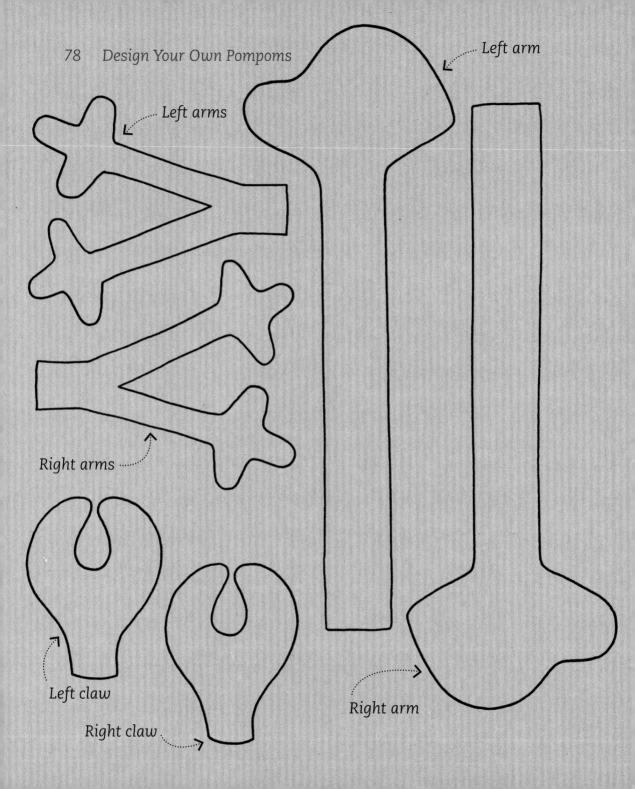

Left arm

Left arms

Right arms

Left claw

Right claw

Right arm

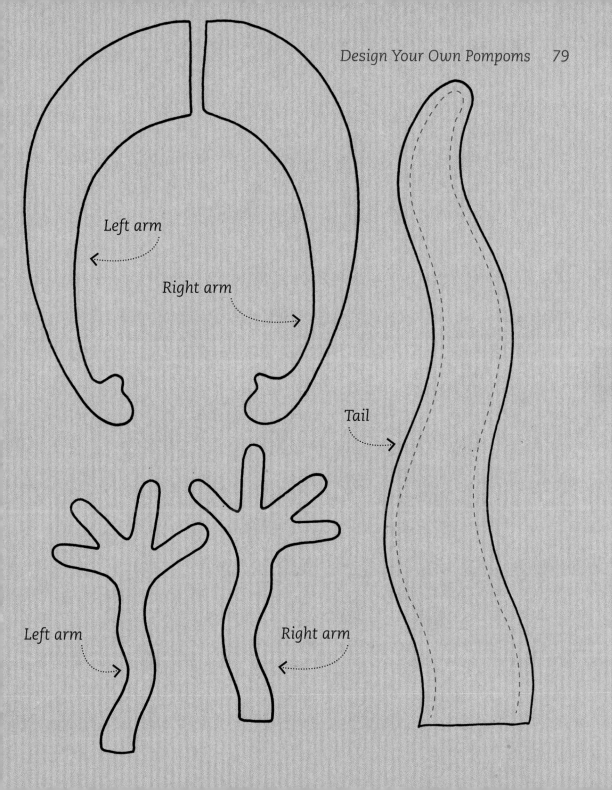

Left arm

Right arm

Tail

Left arm

Right arm

INDEX